HAL LEONARD
harmonica
SERIES

COUNTRY FAVORITES
arranged by DAN FOX

Contents

HAL•LEONARD
CORPORATION
7777 W. BLUEMOUND RD. P.O. BOX 13819 MILWAUKEE, WI 53213

Foreword

This book makes harmonica arrangements of many wonderful Country Favorites available for the first time. A unique feature is the double numbering system through which the songs are playable on either chromatic or diatonic (blues harp) harmonicas. If you play blues harp use the arrows and the upper set of numbers in italic type. Chromatic harmonica is played from the arrows and the lower set of numbers in roman type.

An up arrow (↑) means blow - a down arrow (↓) means draw.

In the diatonic arrangements every note is in the C scale except B♭. B♭ is played by drawing hard on the B natural and forcing the tone down a half step. This is notated by a ⑦.

Sharps and flats in chromatic harmonica arrangements are played by pushing the slide in. This is noted by a circled number.

To play with vibrato (vib.) wave the cupped hand around the harmonica to get an expressive, gently undulating sound.

Each song in this folio is complete. This format, including words, traditional music notation and chord symbols makes it possible for guitar and keyboard players to create accompaniments and for singers to "sing-along".

Smoky Mountain Rain

by KYE FLEMING
and DENNIS MORGAN

Elvira

by DALLAS FRAZIER

Hey, Good Lookin'

by HANK WILLIAMS

9

I Can't Help It
(If I'm Still In Love With You)

by HANK WILLIAMS

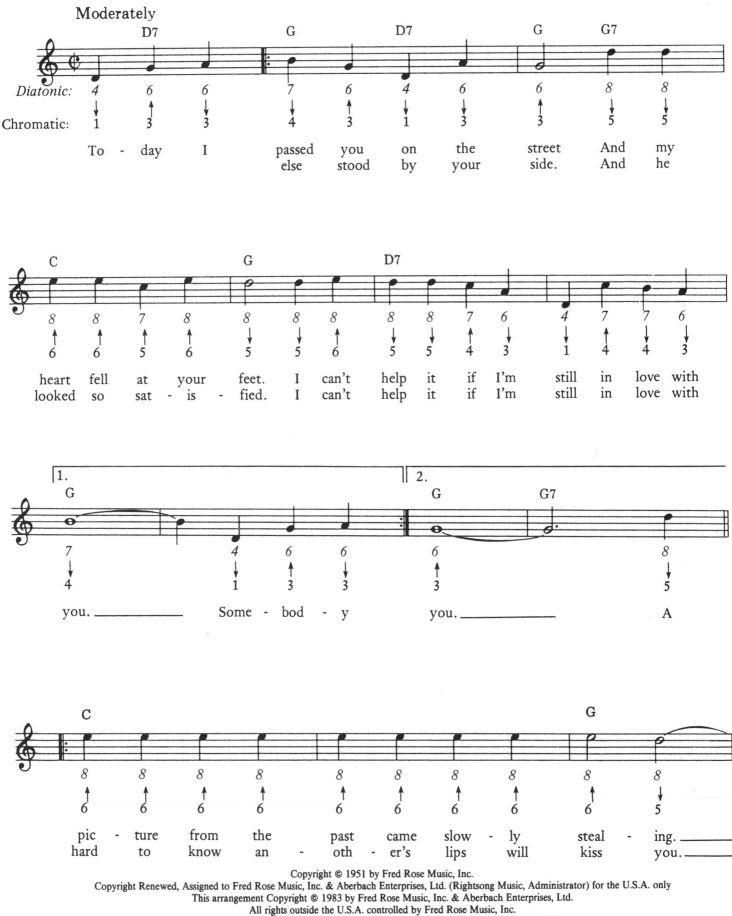

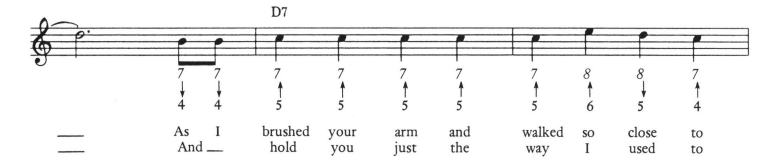

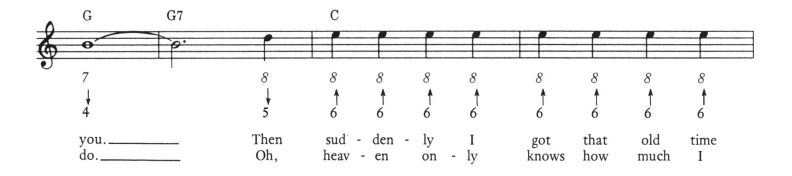

As I brushed your arm and walked so close to
And hold you just the way I used to

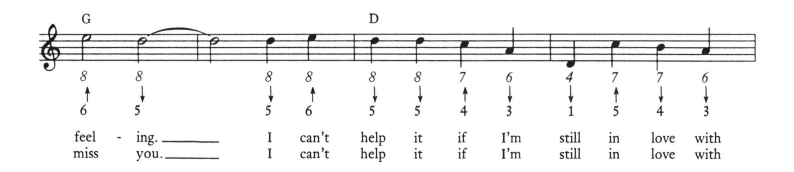

you._____ Then sud - den - ly I got that old time
do._____ Oh, heav - en on - ly knows how much I

feel - ing._____ I can't help it if I'm still in love with
miss you._____ I can't help it if I'm still in love with

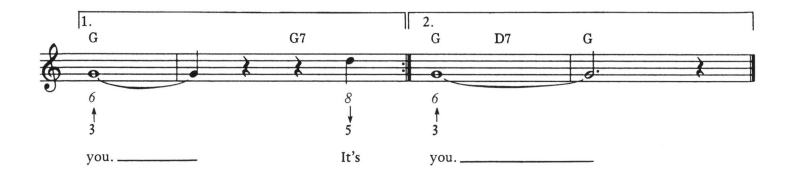

you._____ It's you._____

Your Cheatin' Heart

by HANK WILLIAMS

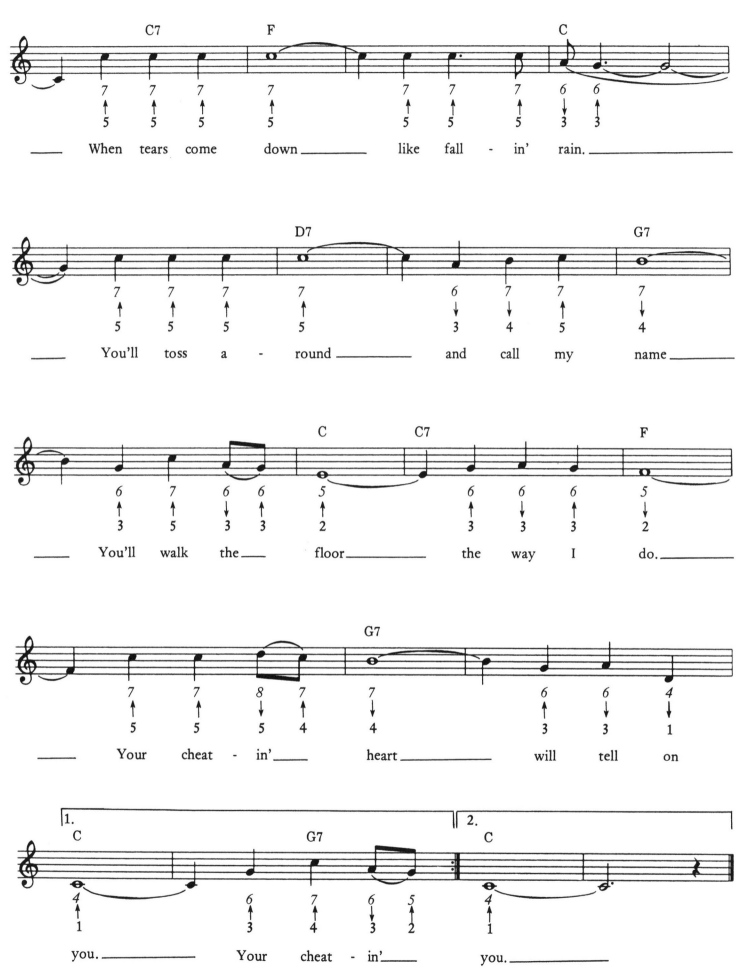

Jambalaya
(On The Bayou)

by HANK WILLIAMS

It's Hard To Be Humble

by MAC DAVIS

Oh, Lonesome Me

by DON GIBSON

I Almost Lost My Mind

by IVORY JOE HUNTER

Green Green Grass of Home

by CURLY PUTMAN

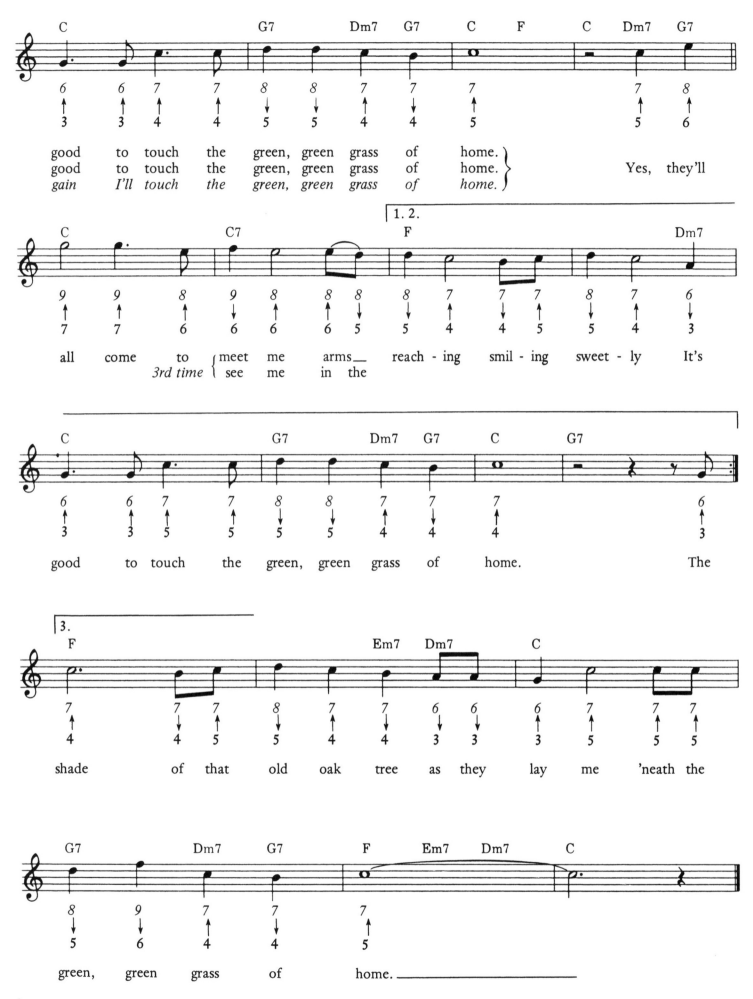

El Paso

by MARTY ROBBINS

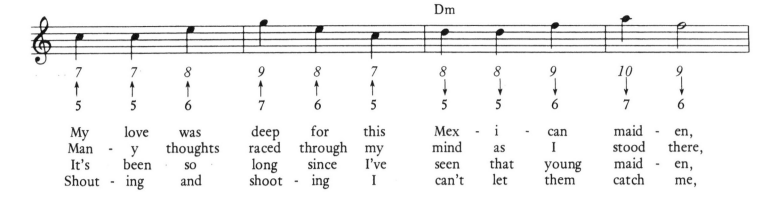

My love was deep for this Mex - i - can maid - en,
Man - y thoughts raced through my mind as I stood there,
It's been so long since I've seen that young maid - en,
Shout - ing and shoot - ing I can't let them catch me,

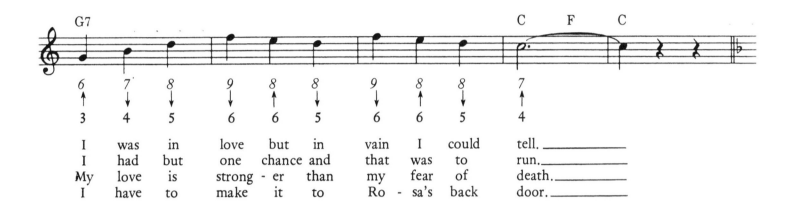

I was in love but in vain I could tell. _____
I had but one chance and that was to run. _____
My love is strong - er than my fear of death. _____
I have to make it to Ro - sa's back door. _____

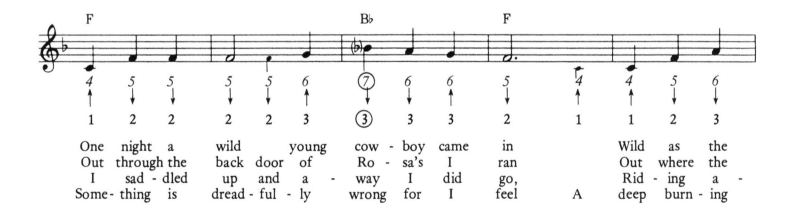

One night a wild young cow - boy came in Wild as the
Out through the back door of Ro - sa's I ran Out where the
I sad - dled up and a - way I did go, Rid - ing a -
Some - thing is dread - ful - ly wrong for I feel A deep burn - ing

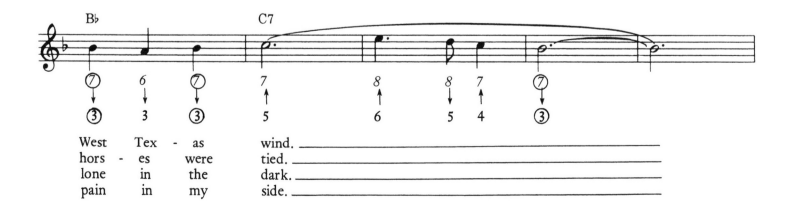

West Tex - as wind. _____
hors - es were tied. _____
lone in the dark. _____
pain in my side. _____

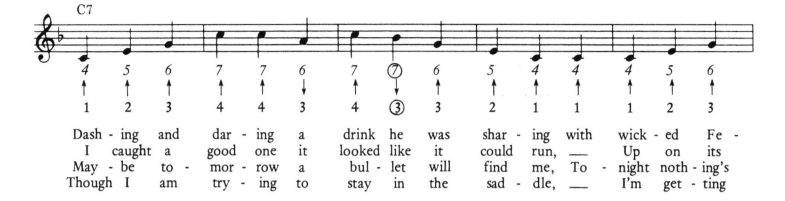

Dash - ing and dar - ing a drink he was shar - ing with wick - ed Fe -
I caught a good one it looked like it could run, ___ Up on its
May - be to - mor - row a bul - let will find me, To - night noth - ing's
Though I am try - ing to stay in the sad - dle, ___ I'm get - ting

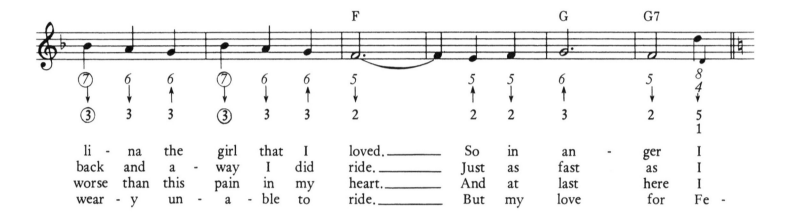

li - na the girl that I loved. _____ So in an - ger I
back and a - way I did ride. _____ Just as fast as I
worse than this pain in my heart. _____ And at last here I
wear - y un - a - ble to ride. _____ But my love for Fe -

chal - lenged his right for the love of this maid - en,
could from the West Tex - as town of El Pas - o,
am on the hill o - ver - look - ing El Pas - o,
li - na is strong and I rise where I've fall - en,

Down went his hand for the gun that he wore. _____ My
Out to the bad - lands of New Mex - i - co. _____ (Solo)
I can see Ro - sa's can - ti - na be - low. _____
Though I am wear - y I can't stop to rest. _____

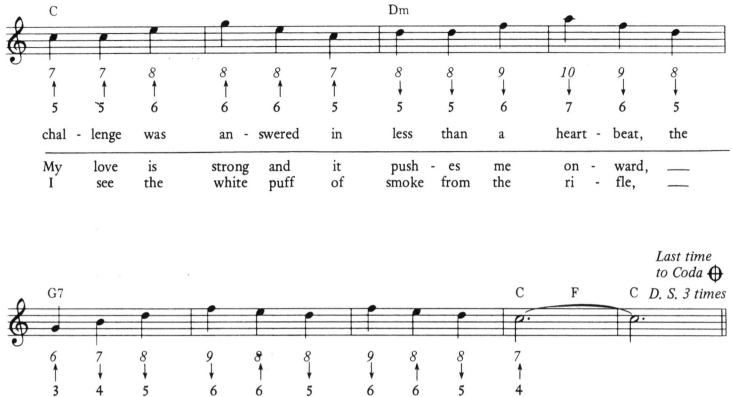

chal - lenge was an - swered in less than a heart - beat, the
My love is strong and it push - es me on - ward, ___
I see the white puff of smoke from the ri - fle, ___

Last time to Coda

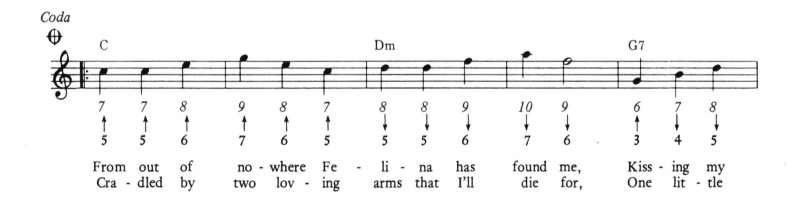

hand - some young stran - ger lay dead on the floor._____
Down off the hill to Fe - li - na I go._____
I feel the bul - let go deep in my chest._____

Coda

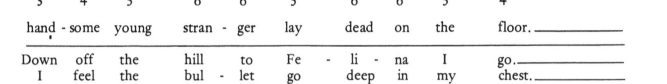

From out of no - where Fe - li - na has found me, Kiss - ing my
Cra - dled by two lov - ing arms that I'll die for, One lit - tle

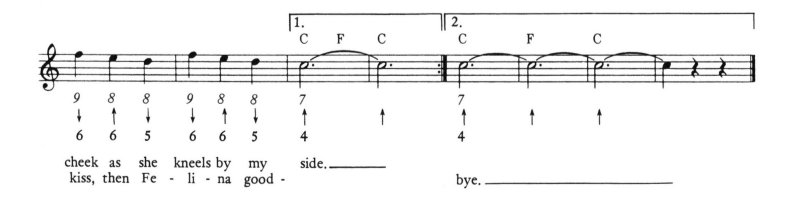

cheek as she kneels by my side._____
kiss, then Fe - li - na good - bye._____

Paper Roses

Words by JANICE TORRE
Music by FRED SPIELMAN

Could I Have This Dance

by BOB HOUSE and
WAYLAND HOLYFIELD

Somebody's Always Saying Goodbye

by BOB McDILL

You Don't Know Me

by CINDY WALKER
and EDDY ARNOLD

Moderate slow shuffle (♩♩♩♩ = ♩. ♩♩. ♩)

G7   C   C7

Diatonic:	6	6	6	6	6	6	6	4	5	6	6	6	7	7	7
	↑	↑	↓	↓	↑	↓	↑	↑	↑	↓	↑	↓	↑	↓	↑
Chromatic:	3	3	3	3	3	3	3	1	2	3	3	3	4	4	4

You give your hand to me ____ and then you say hel - lo, ____ And I can

F   F#o   C   A7

8	7	7	4	5	6	8	7	7	7	6	6	6	6	6	5	6	6
↓	↑	↑	↑	↓	↓	↓	↑	↑	↑	↓	↓	↓	↑	↑	↑	↓	↑
5	5	5	1	2	3	5	4	4	4	3	3	3	3	3	2	3	3

hard - ly speak, __ my heart is beat-ing so, ____ And an - y - one could tell ____ you think you

Dm   G7   C   D7   G7

6	5	5	4	4	5	5	5	6	6	6
↑	↓	↓	↓	↓	↓	↓	↑	↑	↑	↓
3	2	2	1	1	2	2	2	3	3	3

know me well, ____ but you don't know me. _____ No, you don't

C   C7   F

6	5	5	5	4	5	6	6	6	7	7	8	8	7	7	4	5	6
↓	↓	↑	↓	↓	↑	↓	↓	↓	↑	↑	↑	↓	↑	↑	↑	↓	↑
3	2	2	2	1	2	3	3	3	5	5	5	5	4	4	1	2	3

know the one ____ who dreams of you at night, __ and longs to kiss your lips, ____ and longs to

F#o   C   A7   Dm   G7

8	7	7	7	7	6	6	6	6	5	6	6	6	5	5	4	4	5
↓	↑	↑	↑	↓	↓	↓	↓	↓	↓	↑	↓	↓	↓	↓	↓	↓	↑
5	4	4	4	4	3	3	3	3	2	3	3	3	2	2	1	1	2

hold you tight. __ To you I'm just a friend, __ that's all I've ev - er been, ____ but you don't

Stand By Me

by BEN E. KING, JERRY LEIBER
and MIKE STOLLER

Blueberry Hill

by AL LEWIS, LARRY STOCK
and VINCENT ROSE

Bye Bye, Love

by BOUDLEAUX and FELICE BRYANT

Moderate Rock

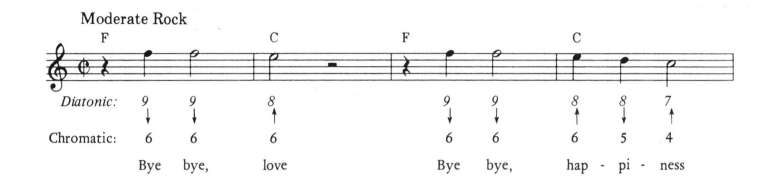

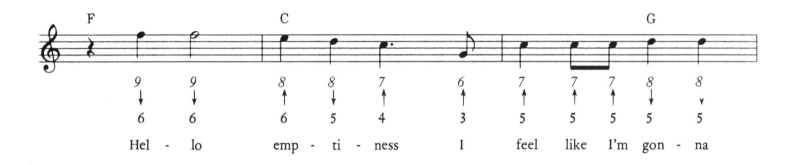

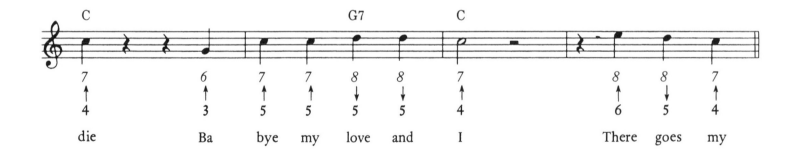

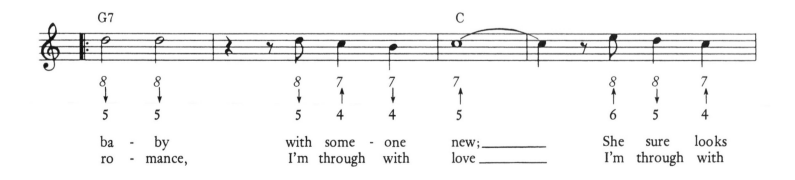

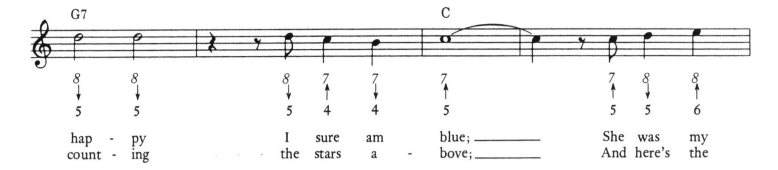

hap - py   I sure am   blue; _____   She was my
count - ing   the stars a - bove; _____   And here's the

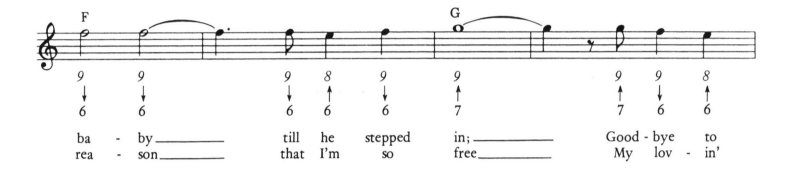

ba - by _____   till he stepped in; _____   Good - bye to
rea - son _____   that I'm so free _____   My lov - in'

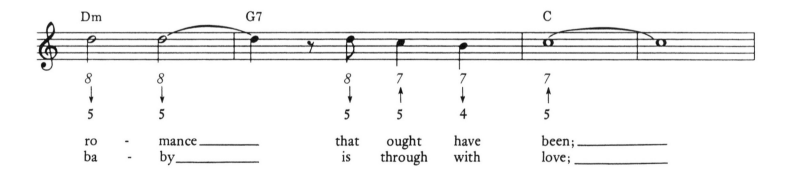

ro - mance _____   that ought have been; _____
ba - by _____   is through with love; _____

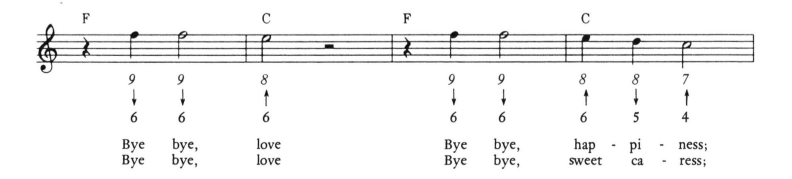

Bye bye, love   Bye bye, hap - pi - ness;
Bye bye, love   Bye bye, sweet ca - ress;

44

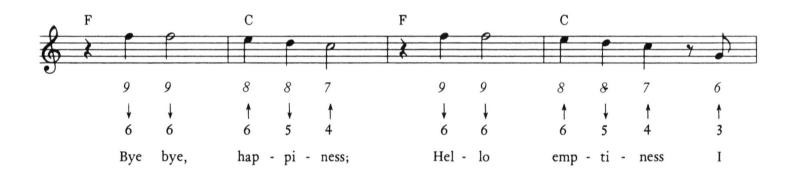

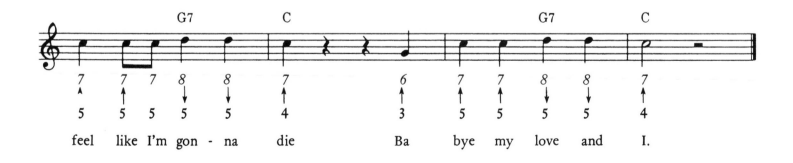

Mammas Don't Let Your Babies Grow Up To Be Cowboys

by ED and PATSY BRUCE

G7

9 9 8 8 8 8 8 7 7 6 6 8 9 9
6 6 6 5 6 6 6 4 4 3 3 6 7 7

nev - er stay__ home, and they're al - ways a - lone, E - ven with

C   G7

8 8 8 7 7 9 9 8 10 9 8 10 9 6
6 6 5 4 4 7 7 6 7 7 6 7 7 3

some - one__ they love.   A

C   C7

8 9 9 10 9 9 8 8 8 9 8 8 8
6 7 7 7 7 6 6 6 6 6 6 5 5

cow - boy ain't eas - y to love and he's hard - er__ to
cow - boy loves smok - y ole pool rooms and clear moun - tain

F   G7

7 7 7 (7) 6 7 (7) 6 5 8 8 9 9 9 9
4 4 4 (3) 3 3 (3) 3 2 5 6 6 6 6 6

hold.   And it means more to him to
morn - ings.   Lit - tle warm

                                                C

9 9 8 8 7 7 7 7 6 6
6 6 6 5 4 4 5 4 3 3

give you a song than sil - ver or gold.
pup - pies and chil - dren and girls of the night.

Love Me Tender

by ELVIS PRESLEY
and VERA MATSON